Ryoanji

At the Ryoanji Temple in Kyoto, Japan, is a garden five hundred years old containing fifteen stones of varying sizes. The floor of the garden is covered with gravel which is raked in straight lines except where it approaches a stone; then it is raked around the stone.

Nothing grows in the stone garden except moss, which grows very slowly.

Ryoanji

Poems by

Tim Reynolds

Harcourt, Brace & World, Inc.

New York

first edition

Library of Congress Catalog Card Number: 64-11539

Printed in the United States of America

Some of the poems in this volume originally appeared in *The
Anagogic and Paideumic Review, The Antioch Review, The Atlantic Monthly, Beatitude, The Beloit Poetry Journal, The Christian
Century, Coastlines, College English, The Critic, Elizabeth, Epoch,
Firebird, Galley Sail Review, The Humanist, Massachusetts Review,
The Midwest, The Nation, New Campus Writing No. 2, New Orleans Poetry Journal, Pan, Poetry, Poetry Northwest, Quagga,
Quixote, Radix, The Reporter, San Francisco Review, Saturday
Review, The Southwest Review, The Sparrow, Tuftonian,* and *The
Virginia Quarterly Review.*

"The Stone-Mason" was reprinted in *The Critic* by Brother Antoninus in his article "A Tribute to Robinson Jeffers." "Potemkin:
Homage to Sergei Eisenstein" and "Heisenberg Variations" appeared
in *Unterwegs,* with German translations by Hubert Gottschling.
"An Allusion to Bendo" is copyright © 1960 by The National Council of Teachers of English.

CONTENTS

Difficulties of a Birdhouse Builder	3
What it is is	4
The Illuminati	5
Sonnets à Hélène	6
To Parsifal, Long After	8
Fable of the Faithful Fisherman	9
Three Translations	11
To a Bad Heart	12
Delos	14
The Stone-Mason	15
Tar	17
Epiphany at Gades	18
Carole	19
A Noiseless Patient	21
Impostures i: Border Guard, Manchuria	22
Impostures ii: Deirdre Young	23
Impostures iii	24
Photograph of a Late Poet	25
Vacuum	26
To a Tree That Damn Near Killed Him	27
Evening	28
The Milkman's Side of Things	29
Janet: 2nd cycle; 1	30
The Winter's Tale	31

After the First Death   32

An Allusion to Bendo   33

The Beaufort Scale   35

Fragment of a Homeric Hymn   36

The long-estranged   37

After Breton   38

The Astronaut   39

Galatea   40

On a Dirty Photograph   41

The First Sorrow of Joseph   43

Recording   44

Hagiograph   45

Potemkin: Homage to Sergei Eisenstein   49

Beautiful creatures   50

Heisenberg Variations   52

Ryoanji   53

The Wave   55

Poem for Hermann Hesse   57

A Walk in March   58

Ryoanji

DIFFICULTIES OF A BIRDHOUSE BUILDER

I swear to God I buy the best wood,
saw it skillfully, plane and sand it down just so,
bevel it lovingly, assemble the pieces
precisely, conscientiously countersink each nail,
and paint everything with the best paint.
I do the best I can. Still and all, though,
the touchy and irrational cardinals for the most part
shun them, and the shy wrens;
not even jays will touch them, or crows, not to speak of
penguins, or vultures. It is incomprehensible.
My house and yard are cluttered everywhere
with these superbly constructed birdhouses,
ornate, immaculate, inanimate—of which,
such as they are, those with some authentic accrual
of genuine bird dung, Ward, I deed to you, in
perpetuity to your heirs and assigns.

WHAT IT IS IS

stone, a pebble, pounded
on abrasive beaches, by waves' torsion
splintered, ground, polished to this small perfection,
which burst unchanneled from a stoppered boil;
after ages' tumbling its chilly
weight warms to my hand.

What lust the hands take
in hefting so and fondling such shapes,
the eyes divining infinity of grace
in simple finite things; as a Danish bowl's
contours from its thin turned lip
rise; it too was rock,

rock worn down deeper still
than in my hand this stone, crushed
to sand, amorphous and diffuse—but healed,
gathered in flame, by deft tools touched,
holds itself again annealed,
focus of light, hushed.

Stone gives and keeps at once.
Far from any sea, take in your hands
earth, from which our dying green forms rise:
before the seas' long pummeling, and the rains',
think, all this gravid dirt was stone!
Stone: what it is, is.

THE ILLUMINATI

Nine years come winter come summer Bodhidharma sat
in Wei in diamond mudra before a wall
and when he stood stood shadowless; as visible grace
his shadow, locked to the stone like ivy, stayed,
a black coat on a hook. It happens as simply as that.

For illumination is effortless when it comes, easy
as a fossil's eternity in a men's room, frozen
in a stone slab—six ribs chevroned, a duck-flock, each
perfect. That creature never tried, simply lay down
in precambrian mud and pulled the eons over its head;
sleeps radiant now through generations of unscanned ephemera
                                                    and
filthy pictures—inarticulate urge of some animal
aching for a personal forever—swiped off daily
by a bored janitor's damp rag.

And illumination came suddenly, effortlessly, to some few
who expecting nothing particular on that day
on that Hiroshima street
sensed Apocalypse bulging from Heaven like an absolute
                                        answer,
unspeakable, instantaneous—where I have seen their shadows,
locked in concrete,
floating leaflike in the lake ice of a hard winter.

SONNETS À HÉLÈNE
(after Ronsard)

i.

These winter nights, these long nights, when the moon
pivots, a death's-head, dead side toward me always,
when semis and sonic booms wake me to nothing new,
I smoke and drink too much, lie brass-mouthed and bilious
alone, lady, and might, for want of you,
have died, as poets threaten, but don't—like me
they can work it off handily on a spook;
she comes to me in shape of you nightly.
In point of fact, you haven't the slightest interest
in sharing my bed. This spook, however, has—
and has moreover a lively imagination,
denying me nothing. She says and does what you ought.
Sometimes I think I'm better off. What is
a poet to do? drink? He's got to love someone.

ii.

Charles himself shrieked 'Kill!,' plugged passersby
with an arquebus, France rives wide with war,
and I lisp love. Less lunatic than I
the manacled certified writhe in their dung-stiff straw.
Rickety, black- and stump-toothed, I splay my soul
in verse to an ice-blooded neoplatonic bitch
whose animus floats in a veil of nasty flesh,
drivel and brood while the old world goes to hell—
Henri collects mignons and Pekinese
and wouldn't know Poetry if it buggered him
in broad daylight, and I, Prince of Pimps, eulogize
him and you, and you gabble third-hand Plato. . . .
Time slips, lady, time slips; dawn's dewy blossoms
rot by nightfall: be mortal now, immortal later.

iii.
That day in Catherine's geometrical
pleasaunce, the Tuileries, the rosemary
was clipped to gargoyle shapes as if to parody
breathing humanity. I grew heretical,
pleading the body's suit—as though a spark
of feeling should creep into some mechanical
sonnet of Desportes', something maniacal
and flawed. Lady, that moment I saw the park
animated, its palisades of box,
privet and jasmine burn with life, become
for that moment unsymmetrical, those labyrinths
of rigid elms and sycamores soften, relax,
grow to us. And you stiffened as if you'd seen
a dogturd or a carcass in your path.

TO PARSIFAL, LONG AFTER
For R S

I can see how it was. Betrayed
by blood and muscle, finding even your instincts
inoperable, lethal, forbidden or irrelevant,
you went partly haywire, as when the back guns,

misinformed, shell the front troops; you
became about half human. Although the dog-
collar around your loins had worn a hairless groove
and with your tail you handled your chain as deftly

as a grande dame her train, the graft never took;
you were not sufficiently human. I have
a wife now, and a son, and two
white rats named Argorotox' and Smintheus

(you would have bitten them all, Parsifal) but still
miss you, remembering your pinched old man's face
and the soft black palms of your hands,
like a baby's, with minute nails; remembering

how you howled, free for once, on a back fence,
gibbering crazily in the terror and bewilderment
of chainlessness, not going far from me but refusing, too,
to return—even for love or bananas.

FABLE OF THE FAITHFUL FISHERMAN

Not that he wasn't happy enough under the sea
with his caudate doxy, his adorable finned sweet
(glaucous the lower moiety, head burnished bronze,
a perpetual Christmas): festooned richly in kelp-fronds,
tended by sylphlike angelfish, entertained by a fleet
of dolphins, guided, guarded by sharks and morays, he

was happy enough; still, after a time he longed to see his home,
just for a day, and moped through the rainbow-coral corridors
distracted until his unhappy undine gave in at last,
seeing she could not hold him even by heaven: "If you must,
you must," she said; "take this for token," weeping her salt
tears
into the salt ocean, foreseeing how she would wait and he not
come,

ever, like all the other fishermen; "but you must not
open it, on peril of your return"—and she swam with him
to the very margin of the waves before she turned with a flirt
of her tail home. And the fisherman, cumbrous on dirt—
how heavy his limbs seemed!—, an uncouth Venus from the
foam,
strolled dripping up the path to the long-time longed-for
hamlet

and found it, of course, altered beyond all knowing; toyed
with the box (an exquisite thing: chased silver, pearl-laced,
locked with a dainty clasp he could have snapped one-handed)
but fought down (unique among fishermen, so fully enchanted
he was) his itching fingers, and by this released
at last from all bond to death and earth and humankind

from a sea-brink promontory plunged and jubilant among
starfish and sea-urchins rollicked weightlessly home to his
                                                    waiting
merlove, who fervently bussed him; but first took back her
                                                       box.
When he asks (having passed his Test) what was in it, she
                                                      talks
of something else: "Nothing," she says, or "Kiss me, darling."
He worries. It's not like it was, he thinks, as if something were
                                                     wrong.

THREE TRANSLATIONS

i.

My woman is Arkheanassa of Kolophon
  in whose each wrinkle smoulders a bitter love.
You young men who shipped on her maiden voyage,
  out of what conflagration you have come!

                              (Plato)

       ii.
       Dusk, you gather, gather all home, all
           splendid dawn scattered—
           lamb, kid you gather, child
               to the mother home.
                              (Sappho)

iii.

No longer, Timaria, the planks of your once
  trim skiff bear Cypris' strokes yarely.
Your back slopes like a lopped yardarm;
  raveling, your halyards hang slack.
Those lax breasts dangle like dropped sails
  harboring; your hold sloshes with bilge-
water where the sea whelms you below, your
  rotten timbers go loose and sundering
with age. Unhappy who, in a tub so like to founder,
  makes, quick yet, for Acheron's dank havens.
                              (Meleager)

TO A BAD HEART

Speak, thou jaded heart, defective heart,
heart kneaded with cold water, scraggy heart,
short-winded heart, devourous heart, hooked heart,
ass-ridden, over-lechered, plucked-up heart,
bestunk, maleficated, lumpish, prolix
heart, heart, heart, beblistered, seedless, void:
What will you promise now? Last time you swore—
remember? in the barn?—things would be different;
but nothing's ever different. And I'm fed up.
Get out! This time I swear I'm serious. Heart,
I've longed to see you dead. I've dreamed of you
cold as a cow's heart in a butcher's showcase
jutting your battleship big guns, a beef-chunk
blood-drained, koshered, pure. I tell you, heart,
you World's Most Perfectly Developed Heart,
bottlecap-bender unable to touch your ear,
armpit-razored oiled bronze bulging hulk,
those flabby fairy hearts that whistle at you
are such as kick chairs in their scrawny rage,
frustrated, pimply, adolescent hearts
who know you only on the comic covers
posed like a rock of muscle. Oh, I have seen you,
heart, yes you, you Cardiac Giant, cringe
before a simple heart one-half your size,
solaced you dragging your bruised auricles home,
aorta between your legs like a booted dog,
snivelling of some gang of bullies. Sero
te amavi, tough but O so gentle.
Compare those swollen ventricles with the hard
lissome chambers of any healthy heart,
grown through those flexions natural to hearts
tough and able to take care of itself,

not bloated like a vacuumcleaner-bag
with strained, incessant, unnatural exercise.
You ought to be ashamed, you hear me, heart?
What did I do to deserve a heart like you?

DELOS

They took away all sepulchres whatsoever of such as had died there before; and for the future, made an edict that none should be suffered to die, nor any woman to bring forth child in the island.

Sun sprawls heavily over white walls. In the square
at a fountain four women wash clothes; the smack
of wet linen on worn stone ricochets
through the streets like small-arms fire. Racket
of agora, dull surf-boom, hush here.
    Relax. You're not going anywhere.

The island slopes from a cypress- and cedar-studded
mountain to beaches where the Aegean wears
lazily and endlessly tumbles edgeless rocks.
Boats are hauled up there; cork floats and spread
fish-nets dry in the sun, with oddments of gear.
    Take it easy. Where do you think you are?

Silver-grey olive trees float like a chilly mist
on the steep rises. Sheep stray untended. At dawn
fishermen leave the rock—and at nightfall, raucous, drunk
with work, resinous wine, sea-heave, dump their still spastic-
ally flailing catch on the sand, a hoard of silver.
    There is nowhere to go: no you to go there.

THE STONE-MASON

*The stone-mason seeketh for work in all manner of hard
stone.
When he hath finished it his arms are destroyed, and he is
weary. . . .*

Lying on sand where mountain streams break through, I have
seen
at night, on bridges, streaks of black across the burning stars,
headlights; whose light, passing the concrete slats, quite suddenly
shut like a fan: driving the high cliff road, coming slowly
around
a granite shoulder, I saw once a comber of white fog poised
so like a wave, so huge, so heavily, that I stopped the car,
braced
for the fall: I have watched hawks in updraft effortlessly lifting,
wings wide: seen redwoods' strength and cypresses' warped
endurance;
sea-carved granite headlands plumbing sheer down, bicep-
curved, to sea;
half-seen deer—seen, but never freshly, all this having been
claimed by
him who staked out this land, these permanences, unalienably
for his.

And I have seen him, who quarried out and worked this raw
existence,
the stone-mason: seen him walking by day in shade of the big
trees
framing the tower of boulders he hung against the sky, back
broad
and hard-handed—but bent, but slow, after a spent life of
building

something more lucid than any visible light, lighter than fog,
lifting still higher than hawk-flight, yet comprehending most
                                                              things
hard, pure and durable, something tough as backbones of coas-
                                                          tal hills
and spacious, like a tower, with a solid place to stand on top—
watched him picking his way along rock shores at night, alone
under the stars he loves (which, weary now, burn steadily,
                                                            if far,
fragments of an older fury).

                                                    Nepenthe, 1958

TAR

Night closes down
          on thirteen barrels and
one bird and two board hoppers filled with sand;
a green tangle
          of weeds has overgrown
the lot, wild as a jungle.

The bird, its belly-
          cage a crib of twigs,
its feathers splayed about it like frayed rags,
lies on its back
          in a shiny pool of spilled
tar, where it landed, and stuck.

Almost you hear
          the howling of trapped beasts
holding fast to their fat prey, held fast,
the eaters eaten
          by the blind sucking tar.
The bird, I think, sat down

just to get warm.
          If you place a stone on top
of that slick surface, it will be enveloped
ever so slowly,
          though it still seems firm:
a nightmare of long falling,

implacable, slow—
          and you'll find it, if you pass
tomorrow, flat as Alice's looking glass,
obsidian-blank.
          The stone, perhaps, although
dead still, still sinks.

EPIPHANY AT GADES
For J J

We got sick and tired of the whole business
after a week—cat-squalls, scooter-whine, blind
men hollering lottery tickets.
It wasn't the real thing after all,
not even boys singing with guitars on the streets,
not even the yellow-bulbed Catedrál
bonging the days' demarcations over the racket,
or bluebottles clustering on meat in the mercado.
It wasn't what we were after; we might as well
have stayed home.
              It only came clear finally
when we had taken off, when the snarl of streets
simplified like a complex
equation to the blunt republican
X, the castra's fossil crux,
real as could be, even if beyond the vallum
the oblong frayed out, became ambiguous,
until we couldn't say quite where Sein stopped being.

Still farther, over the ocean,
Cadiz became only a speck, if that—
and then we saw how even the mountain-spines
and coastline zagged down like many coordinates
of one event,
X-ing the very spot.

CAROLE

After bladeprobe,
binding, unbinding, weeks in bed,
final decision: Blind.
And staring dully out of her stone head,

claysocketed,
she comes to know the dark. Things
threaten; only her fingers'
touch, arms' span, fend off suspected

hurt, collect a
real encompassable world where safe
she moves among known
furniture, from bed to chair to telephone,

or talks with friends,
a smile clenching and unclenching
on her face under the greenbrown
glasses, each glance a wince, gesture a flinching

from collision.
The touch of no flesh, she finds,
penetrates her really,
the grope and clasp of bodies grants no vision

(a second's glimpse
of wall, pillow, ashtray, clock,
would be a vision); she takes
bodies like hands, something to hold in the dark.

She begins to note
her memory bleaching out ('Red was
the violent color?'), judges
voices more than words, hands more than voices,

thought least: waits
that love refracted in her stony
sockets may build in her skull
at last a something sensible, a world like light.

A NOISELESS PATIENT

Through a whole living room and half across
a back yard one strand of spiderweb caught sun
as trees dropped away under, stretched taut between
two spruce branches; whether more or less
than miracle I can't say, that burning point-wide line:
starlike it was all light, and bodyless.

Straight as seam or sea horizon, faultlessly it
gathered to it and split everything
or, as if comprehending the whole morning,
bounded it mathematically. I tell you I sat
watching sick as any the banjo-tight
blond hemp stiff and quivering from trap just sprung

so long as that angle of eye and sun hung fire—
quenched, it crumbled like the dead queen's hair.

IMPOSTURES I:
BORDER GUARD, MANCHURIA

Mortar-set fireplace stones;
straight-grained half-charred
woodchunk, cross-scored;
wine-gallon; hatchet;
books; pipe; matches;
silent telephone—
from my doorsill, fog,
pines in receding planes
as through a steamy pane
a strange crowd, dark faces.

IMPOSTURES II:
DEIRDRE YOUNG

As dust-mote in sun-spoke
climbs, as in quiet air
smoke rises, so Deirdre grew,
drifting and eddying through
familiar chambers, golden mornings,
formal gardens, upborne
by warm currents beyond
her casual unthinking:
how, in such clarity,
foresee and fear
that floating smoke
might curdle in the beam,
sun be, one sad dawn,
unrising, known rooms darken,
dust, unheld, sink down?

. . . thou wentest
after me in the
wilderness, in a
land that was not
sown . . .

Sun, burn,
sand, scour,
o ream me clean
of this, this flesh,
this adamant
banana-rotten
body's weight:
abrade, chastise,
shear me,
fierce sand;
intolerable sun,
scald flay
fray decay despoil
destroy
o all
but soul of me.

PHOTOGRAPH OF A LATE POET

Stranger to me, even then he was unworlding—
   not as you are, in whom death hangs
motionless, lazily finning barracuda-fashion,
   but swiftly as coffee subverts a sugar-lump,
infiltrating him while he posed even, crumbling
   the cooling fingers around the still warm pipe.
Like the woman camera-caught in the morning papers
   midway down from parapet to concrete
he is held falling in this imponderable halflife
   as though at swordpoint over a black blood trench
across which what can I ask but the ordinary question:
   Did having dealt a lifetime with this matter
make those minutes easier when in the brain space
   collapsed upon itself, then ripped apart,
supernova, throat turned sphincter? Posed, frozen,
   the eyes like poems smile and answer nothing.

VACUUM

AS under belljar the stridently clattering
  alarmclock's rage dulls to a tinny
    buzz, and silence (save sibilance
    of airpump) dead to a deaf sense,
  though beneath the exhausted dome the tiny
hammer is furiously soundlessly continuously beating,

      SO after violence—
  hand come bloody away from
  belly; wheels still stupidly revolving;
  soft echoes of detonation bumbling
    about—is suddenly nothing,
    in that peculiar silence,

to breathe: nothing to do; under the glass dome
    all is unmoving, unbreathing
    (save a frantic unheard clattering:
the heart furiously soundlessly continuously beating).

TO A TREE THAT DAMN NEAR KILLED HIM
(after Horace)

Whoever, one black Friday the Thirteenth,
planted you here, and raised you from a sapling
to be a boobytrap for strolling poets,
the scandal and disgrace of the neighborhood,

whoever it was, there's nothing I'd put past him:
arson, childrape—bagatelles to that man
who put you in my field, you lousy log,
where Nestor-wise you passed up three generations

and died, and rotted, and yesterday fell on me.
One is never sufficiently circumspect
concerning death. How many who feared torpedoes
and kamikazes three years in the Pacific

have been run over, drunk on shoreleave, by taxis?
How many, dreading sudden annihilation
in nuclear holocaust, more dolefully
perish of hiccups, bee-stings, drown in toilets?

Death is always ridiculous; always one jump
ahead; always an occupational hazard
for poets, who must write as best they can
under excessively trying circumstances.

EVENING

Heavy and everywhere the smell
of lilacs
permeates the apartment. My wife leaned
from our secondfloor window and cut them
with scissors. Spring swamps
us—penetrating drains,
light sockets, the recesses
of closets, the cramped
mind. Lilacs!
I lean back and breathe deep.

THE MILKMAN'S SIDE OF THINGS

Delivering milk at night in the Bronx he sees
pressed into doorways and still as marble or bronze,
beyond the reach of light and the days' demands,
dark figures blended and shaped to darkness. These

are lovers, blind, who only know through touch,
whose vestigial eyes are marbles in their heads
but whose hands are warm and soft.
                                        Venereal blood
swells to the shingles of their hearts, where such

blind pulsing rails such violence to their palms
as day cannot conceive. Then shuddering
their flesh accords to the blood's *Belong   Belong*,
swells and gathers and bursts.
                                        Then there is calm,

and then the night is silent, and the streetlamps fail,
and the wet lovers cling in a welter of sweat and breath,
arched in a brownstone doorway, and beneath
their hands are gentle in their nightlong Braille.

But for the milkman alone on the void streets
the lights are firm and close, and quietly
he rebukes his own blood: *When they meet by day
they do not know. Their hands are out of sight.*

Suffering Aristotle saw stone
like rose or man or state growing toward
entelechy, but in falling, more
   itself as it neared home;

active Alexander sent a Greek
fellow around Arabia to see
if he would drop from or drown in the Oceanus
   where ravening monsters lurked:

but moving or staying, stone's stone,
we know all that; and we know how,
now it's all charted, the world goes round—
   what they understood was heart.

It's heart sails with nothing to steer by
hull down over the safe oikoumene,
pennants stiff and whacking in
   the gale, and over that rim

gape those same nightmares Nearchus feared;
it's heart that, having its own entelechy,
downing and downing from that bound to nullity,
   grows but the more heart.

THE WINTER'S TALE

Ynch-thick, knee deepe; ore head and eares a fork'd one.

Leontes babbles in the draughty halls
and whispers "Horror" from the highest towers
in deadest night, and mutters fitful prayers
heard only by the blank perspiring walls.
What solace for Leontes? As he sleeps
he hears the dusky lovers' voices, wakes,
in dreams, and she is gone, and all the clocks
have stopped, to mock his loss. Her pillow keeps
her head's dark hollow. Then he wakes in sweat
to hear, beyond his rasping gasp for air,
her deep and sleeping breath, and sees some tall
and shadowy lover leave her, and all night
he hides, deep down, in shifting hollows where
he does not know, or can almost forget,
his nightmare twin and twisted self, Sir Smile.

AFTER THE FIRST DEATH

She cried and cried
until her breath was gone. Everyone
wept and they laid her weeping in the ground
and shoveled on the lid.

Her obscure face
congealed in a clenched fist of fear
while her brain screamed *Air!*, a sailor trapped
in the hold of a sinking ship.

The fine canals
of her blood, frozen, closed down
and the tender mesh of nerves like chickenwire
stiffened beneath her skin:

her body died
as a careful housewife before a storm
walks about her home firmly and gently
shutting the windows and doors.

Her hair, seed-like,
pried at the earth a week, then failed.
Her hands grew talons to scrabble at the soil
but they died and turned to roots.

Then nothing stirred
or flinched as beetles probed her wounds
as the philosopher's Tree-in-a-Lonely-Forest
falls without a sound.

AN ALLUSION TO BENDO

The general heads, under which this whole Island
may be considered, are Spies, Buggers, and Rebels;
the transpositions and mixtures of these make an
agreeable variety.
                    John Wilmot, Earl of Rochester

The *Poet*, piecing out his scanty Art,
Corrects the Grammar of th'untutored Heart;
So will the *Whore*, long dead to Love's true fire,
Sob, moan, writhe, clip and pant, appear t'expire
In ecstasy; the *Player* to Heaven throws
His arms, screws up his face, shrieks fit to rouse
The *Furies*—while his quick eyes count the House.
Scorn not my sworn Profession, *Mountebankery;*
There's none but has its taint of Hanky-Pankery,
Not one is Honest: *Politician, Sweep,*
Can both be bought, one dear, the other cheap:
Cheats all; your *Soldiers, Doctors, Lawyers, Car-men*—
But I'll be brief; I'm not to preach a Sermon
(Although I ought to tell you, apropos,
I'd not except those pious dupes who do so).
Then, Sirs & Ladies, castigate who dares;
Not one but has a *Conscience* in arrears—
Consider too: the brave man wears a Sword,
Struts, boasts of Husbands hoaxed and goodwives whored,
Watches belabored, horrid brawls lived through,
Terrific prowess: so does the *Coward* too,
And what's to tell the difference in the two,
Save testing? And cannot a dull *Ass* speak
Judiciously, and stroke his chin, and hawk,
And hem—and who's to say who's *Ass*, who *Clerk?*
While any *Gallant* knows to counterfeit
With purloined songs and perjured sighs and wit

A very *Tristram* or an *Abelard;*
Nor any rustic *Justice* finds it hard
To praise the folk on whom his Place depends,
Call ev'ry Woman *Goddess,* all men Friends,
While groaning (privily), *Ah, Hoi-polloidom,*
I'd give my very Office to avoid 'em.
Scorn not then, *Ladies, Sirs,* the *Mountebank,*
A very humble *Fraud* midst Rank on Rank
Of arrant *Swindlers, Humbugs, Rogues, Knaves,* **Quacks**—
Then let me now unbundle all my knick-knacks,
My *Powers, Salves, Elixirs, Balsams, Pills,*
Ointments, Liniments; Come, bring me your ills,
Tell whatever Ailment long has troubled.
You may find cure, perhaps; or your pain doubled:
It's not the first nor last time you've been bubbled.

THE BEAUFORT SCALE
For Jessica

is outmoded, not precisely indicative
of wind velocity, and so found
only in obsolete nautical textbooks.
It retains, however, a primal significance:
as calibrator of heart's weather it is sound.
CALM it classifies as that spellbound timeless
long afternoon when sparrows
chitter like old wagon wheels and "smoke
goes straight up"; "smoke drifts" in a LIGHT AIR.
In a SLIGHT BREEZE
"leaves rustle". A GENTLE BREEZE
sets "leaves and small twigs . . . in motion".
In a MODERATE BREEZE "dust flies; and paper;
small branches move". Then, in a FRESH BREEZE, "small trees
sway," we note "wavelets on water".
In a LARGE BREEZE
"large branches move; umbrellas are blown".
"Whole trees move; walking is difficult" in a HIGH WIND.
"Twigs break off" in a GALE.
Following these
come the STRONG GALE ("loose shingles and chimneys go"),
WHOLE GALE ("trees may be uprooted"), STORM
("damage is widespread") and last the HURRICANE,
when "anything may go".
When everything is gone,
the mast-stripped battered mariner heart may find
at the embattled winds' eye, waters' center, CALM.

FRAGMENT OF A HOMERIC HYMN
For C O

      . . . no god of drinking song
or bestial women roaming crazed and bloody on the mountain-
                sides
or rouged vinewreathed ephebes, no lute-plucker chanting
stones from their sockets. Leave love and wine and honey-
                words
to their sponsors—for there live those who have heard the
                stony clang
of the silver bow, the whiz and thunk of His shafts; have
                sweated
in gut-terror by the thundertongued sea where the hollow ships
lay beached, and about them pyres grease-smoking, thickset
as mountain pines and pleasanter to His nostrils than fat thighs
of bulls or he-goats; there live those yet who wake home in
                warm bed
with slaves, Ilion-spoil, cold at marrow still, having again
                dreamt
the Mouse-god nibbles at the troops like cheese . . .

tryst on the station platform between trains,
sighting each other down twin windowed rows,
ponderous wheels and weighty shafts. They close
as movie gunmen down an empty street,
falsefronted, stalk inflexible and meet
in violence that explodes intolerable strain.

They dare not pause: and as they move they grow
the very substance of the girding steel.
Seconds clank home like tumblers; and anneal
as rivets tumbled white-hot into holes
cooling swell to bear their shear and skyward thrust.

And then a subtle shifting of the poles

and swiftly, within their lodestone orbs, they leap
and ring together; cinctures coincide
about that center, lash of unleashed springs:
and nothing holds them apart now but skin . . .

as should around some mythy corner creep
Midas and Medusa, and collide,
and turn themselves to gold and stone—a cold
hard basalt block shot through with warmest softest gold.

AFTER BRETON

I have found the secret.
In the world I map
you are those islands of not-me

I raise. And this always outward voyage
of loving you
is, still, finding wherever in mind I make for

my flagship anchored in your windward harbor,
my landing parties out for water now and
always for the first time.

> J'ai trouvé le secret
> de t'aimer
> toujours pour la première fois.

THE ASTRONAUT
For N M

In the small towns of northeast Kentucky
day fails again; the dusty evening light wrestles up
through sumac and dogwood to the smouldering hillcrests,
shadows flow and fill the floorcracks like water—

that was how it was. Almost immortal here, almost a god,
he recalls those evenings; being beyond the moon's sphere
nothing changes now. His steel-chromium-plastic alloy
bubble surrounds him entirely (he its Intelligence

and plugged into it by one billion wires) as moonwise he
falls insistently to earth, like the swung waterbucket
unspilled. Seasons flicker and blur on the tiny planet.
Days and nights fuse. He thinks of northeast Kentucky

as another country, disjunct somehow from that shuttle
of tints on a hung bauble—as Joliet folks, when the lights
dim and brighten, believe it rather something in their eyes
or heads or wiring or fusebox than universe.

And so he becomes a god; he can feel divinity stir in spine
and cortex, amalgamated and apotheosized in copper and steel
and the rest. His mind strolls through the almost eternal hills
of northeast Kentucky and sees its handiwork and finds its
good.

GALATEA

was as any human child conceived
in flesh, but born in stone; she grew,
a tremulous bud, in Pygmalion's hothouse mind
until at last her final form, full-leaved,
stood gazing under his chisel-blows
and came to be complete. The sculptor's tool was stained
with blood, and he, bewildered, touched her neck,
no longer mineral but catalpa-firm.
He stroked her belly. It was warm.
He loved what he had made until in time
he woke to find his mistress again rock.

The streetwalker pounds pavements and becomes
cement; the pelted witch a scarred pebble;
the bombed-under and charred housewife rubble;
bony spinsters mingle with their marble tombs;
the five o'clock women on Fifth Avenue
are brayed to powder in that river's flow:
mineral infiltrates to seize the precious Form
as flesh evaporates.
                    Pygmalion's passion
wilts before her concentric grace, the fern's
fossil lace: refrozen, she returns
no touch or love: he mourns, with his hands' warmth
at her cold breasts, his living breath on the stone mouth
of Galatea poised in pedestaled reversion
to art, her curves geometry
and unapproachable to him as memory.

ON A DIRTY PHOTOGRAPH
For V née S

It was my first Fourth, and over the nightlong water
pollen drifted from scarlet petals, light
   broke on the low waves and sifted
down to the fishes. Sudden thunder clattered
over the glassy bay and rocking boats,
         echoed popcorn soft.

Our shadowy faces flushed red and green in the dark.
I was stunned by the whole extravagance, but later,
   thudding back, sleepy, to the dock,
I leaned over the splintery rail and wondered
which was Real, the gentle and unreflecting water
         or the remembered thunder . . .

Just so I wonder at this cheap photograph.
Supposing my figure sound, which term goes where?
   Should these be considered the husk of love
or its indispensable kernel, fireworks or the sea,
these bored models who pose love's mechanics, bare
         on a hired bed, for a fee?

The question being, which are the pyrotechnics,
the vaunted wordy images, or the furtive act?
   these waxworks, or Heloise and her tonsured eunuch?
In our sportive sonnets do we, with Aretino,
contemplate our own privates merely? plucked,
         do we stew in our own *mana?*

Or do we die and rise in unspeakable passion,
our tides and the waves' one, and fireworks
   of flesh but gaudy intimations
of Reality's combers, ponderous beneath?

In any case, these depths are fraught with sharks
        and topped with devious froth.

As puzzled Tristram, his life past all control,
ceased, so must I, my problem barely posed.
    Still, in this photograph I feel
some paradox impinging on the Real,
would plunge to follow the gleam of a glimpsed rose
in the deeps of that sounding, if unsounded, sea.

THE FIRST SORROW OF JOSEPH

Before her body grew heavy, it grew light.
She moved with a new grace; her ears still rang
with the clamor of her terrible messenger's song;
and when she closed herself for sleep at night
that splendor echoed in her shuttered eyes.

This Joseph knew, who saw her day by day
draw from him as a stone drops down a well;
then saw himself, gesticulating, small,
reflected in the mirrors of her eyes
as in well-water when its ripples die.

And Joseph knew she stood in a bright room
with but one other, and a door between.
How could he understand? He held his peace.
And peace grew still in Mary's quickened womb—
an alien light moved sometimes in her eyes.

RECORDING
For Harry Partch

After the glossy vinylite whirlpool had subsided
dragging to the bottom spars flotsam buoys
sailors bottles floating crates staved-in boats
seawrack—in short after everything there was
after absolutely everything had been caught
in that amazement of water and gone down
then I found myself heaved up on a still shore
under eucalyptus and redwood trees
far from that omniverous ocean
almost foundering again in a silence
even the shrill crickets couldn't drown.

HAGIOGRAPH
For A

1. CHILD IN THE YARD
Behold, I am knocking at the door . . .
He who has an ear, let him hear . . .

Behold, sound the drummed ears in the round head;
Behold, sigh budding flowers from the palate;
Behold, thumps the blood, I am knocking at your heart;
And Urizen from the fissured cloudshaped mind

Thunders Behold; the soft lips, soles and palms,
The somnolent coiled pythons in the bowels,
The egg laughing shyly, locked in the childish belly,
The terrible angel sleeping in the loins,

The sticky fingers and, from the bloody basket,
The cut umbilical choir Behold, Behold—
While out past the sharp pickets Stone cries Heft me!
Air Run in me! Daisy Try my veracity! Sun Make hay!

2. THE FIRST DEBAUCH

Pearshaped urinals choiring round his head
wheel icy with a chill celestial fire;
epicicular stalls and washbowls gyre
singing in their cycles; but the spread-
eagled earth-intelligence—how fallen!—lies
in his vomit, all unsphered, and looks away
from the tiled gleaming Primum Mobile,
the Unmoved Moving, dare not raise his eyes;

lost, abased, alone in this realm of light
he has tasted the Forbidden, and is dark,
flaw in the faultless, unchaste in place of prayer
where even soap-dispensers chant His might.
An occasional disinterested Arch-
angel lurches past, urinates, and leaves him there.

3. THE DIG
   Every dream has at least one point at which
   it is unfathomable; a central point, as it
   were, connecting it with the unknown.

Level II: many potsherds; traces of fire
(a circle of blackened stones, charcoal; we've yet
to date this); fragments of basketwork; a bit
of textile (fabric unknown, weave unfamiliar);
and a skeleton, together with 12 blue beads
and a copper utensil, probably a knife.
III: a gold broach (lost-wax); a bas-relief,
marble, in good shape, of a bull; 6 seeds
(hemp is conjectured) in a leather pouch. IV to V-b
yield only flints (flaked) and potsherds, VI
a grave and percussion flints, with some few flakes.
VII: a single eolith, concerning which we
(my colleague, that is, and myself) have had some contention.
I'm sure it's an artifact.
                    Then nothing.
                              And then stone.

4. DEVIANT

It would not have escaped you that our cures
come about through attaching the libido reigning
in the unconscious. . . . It is in essence a cure
through love.

Into what red hell of frenzy has he come
that three inches of muscle in his wetlipped mouth
turn every lie he seeks to screech to truth
before the thought itself is done? The dumb

dessicated eyes, all moisture long since wrung
forth, plead for omniscience from the smiling
Catechist: Oh God, He should know him, know his reviling
is praise, no yes, black white, his screaming song.

Once more the hose drops. Then dark. Oh think,
he tells himself, stone-blind in daylight now the arcs
are off; something to make Him happy. His mind works
like a jackhammer in sand, caves in—he draws a blank.
The switch snaps. He is suffused in light, wave on wave
of light, hurt, hosed, interrogated: it is love, love.

5. SKYWAY BY SCENICRUISER

For there is yet a little light in men;
Let them walk, let them walk, that the darkness overtake
them not.

That haze in the East is no sunrise but the hungered-,
thirsted-for
City; taillights lead him there, Christ's blood who died
to guide him, drop on drop arcing up the broad

crest he now tops, where the goal bursts before
his greedy eyes like Dante's rose; almost he hears the choir,
greeting him, chiming him home, of the sanctified,
the beatified, the saints, the saved of the City of God.

But clambering down at 31st Street, the flames encase
shrieking Donatists; they are the fires of his killed lust
come home by the back way—ah horrible, how they blaze
up, clutching for his garments; no Roma but worse, worst,
and the passing unsinging faces are of the utterly damned,
irrevocably cursed, dead: he drops stricken to the knees of
                                                    his mind.

6. The Rock

juts hard and male from a plowed field, half awash
in grain, where a glacier let it fall, casually,
as it turned back, surrounded year by year by
shuck and chafe of stiff cornblades, steely hiss
of green wheat.
                    Barley, a stemmed sea-creature,
or forked oats, some farmer can strip down, tumbling
the milky groats in his tough palm, and crumble
the chaff to powder; the blindest part conjectures
a sum to all crops and works of calloused hands,
seeing the dry sheath drift off in the sifting wind,
the meat drop dirtwards.
                            In all that reach of field
only that rock is unplowed, unsown, and will not yield—
though all about it in green hosannas stir toward form,
burst, thrust upward, ripen, fail, that rock stands firm:
    as if that icy tide might rise upon the land
    again, and ease its weight, and bear it home.

POTEMKIN: HOMAGE TO SERGEI EISENSTEIN

Not as oil on stilled water or on canvas
buoys a cathedral's lace façade or floats
prince or placid angel in a stasis
of life resolved and lucent, but as wind-
splintered on choppy water the moon's manface
splays foundering, as lambent

in puddles shiver fragments of broken sky,
rain-pocked and cratered, you give us becoming—
no final thing, fixed in an unchanging
amber, oil, lava, formaldehyde, but daylight lancing into the boxed eyeball,
a split-second when spills

the crowding world into the blood-red
retinal cave, bewildering, inchoate:
when creaking wheel, hung bell, hard fist
raised, blind anguished human face split wide,
smoke-billow, bronze cup, maggot-swarmed side of meat,
assume their roles for just

that moment, with the terrifying inconsequence
of a babybuggy clattering downstairs, sense
pure, not made sense of, life-stuff: that clumsy
steel bulk, the stock-still battleship Potemkin
reflected profound, fractured and immense,
in sea-heave darkly rocking.

BEAUTIFUL CREATURES

grow shabby and graceless
in confinement, too awkwardly stand,
too nervously and sullenly on gross feet pace
the moated or barred bounds
beyond which praise

them their dangerous
eyes and teeth and envy them
their firm limbs and most their fierce strangeness
those who at feeding time
at their brute assuageless

voracity
shudder—stuffed, they stand too
flatly on feet too still, and the glass eyes
in their cotton heads show
self-pity

which even in death
they did not know; the veldt lapped
behind them is too tidy, too smooth;
too stiff the rabbit ripped
wide for truth.

Half-hidden
in tall grasses, mottled by leaf-
shadow, there they run wild and lean, fatten-
ing or, should they not prove
swift, eaten.

There do they leap
terribly at you, as a spur of flame
leaps; but so truly are their beautiful shapes:
say then *They drink at a stream;*
say, *How calm their sleep.*

I am accustomed to unravel you
by the least visible indications. Sleep
whelming you now, eye-tic is vertigo
at its edge, leg-jerk a neuron's hurdle deep
in the head; by these I follow you where you go.

As water seeps into dry loam—for a moment
gleaming shiny and black as obsidian,
then, with a sudden snake-flex, shifting, absent—
you slip from me; like some bewildered man
razor-sliced in a bar-brawl, I still can't

feel a thing but, paralyzed, dare not move.
What more help are the fingers of the blind
man than my "crystalline, hexagonal"? Love's,
snowflake-like, not tactile, fat hand
no help, body no fit tool. Thomas believed,

touching: I cannot touch you now; you are
the hours and air and world I live within
unthinking, as close, strange, involute and far.
Let me, as salt and water mixed in one
are two, come somehow into, around you: there

crystallize me suddenly, precipitate me clear.

RYOANJI

The unseen villagers
    have left their huts, or
just sit inside moping.

The armada is armed,
          lethal,
even in this Sargasso.
          Stay clear.

Mountains hammer up
      through mist;
   these fingers
acknowledge no common hand.

Akeley watched for days
   to take them so. They stand
stuffed, grey, motionless.

"Who gathered the embittered
  together into one society?"

Harvest done, haystacks,
    humped in the frozen fields,
      stiffen into winter.

End game.
      Tense with irresolution
the pattern points
      beyond the pattern.

Tombstones remain after
the marked life has gone to
seed,
illegible.

Beyond the garden,
over a low wall,
cypresses,
alive,
fountain.

But huge, and slower
than winter sap in a stripped
tree, a life stirs here.

There are lives and lives.
These fingers, thrust into Flatland,
affirm one more.

THE WAVE

It swept in, a vast curve, from toward Japan,
head high—standing a good foot taller than
the others—as though it thought the rocks would break
against it or step aside or move on back

as it came on; or else as though destruction
were less a matter of fate than of election.
Climbing the suddenly steepening littoral
slope, it stood up ponderous, judicial,

ominous almost; but delicate: nothing spilled.
It seemed to pause forever; then it fell
and shivered like plate glass on the rock shore.
Boulders fought up through collapsed surf to air

and abstract as quanta, waves, diminishing West
in long arcs, foam-ridged at the crests,
kept moving in as though nothing at all had happened.
But something had: that single wave had ripened,

responsive to far-below contours and wind-shove,
had passed through water it was no more part of
than dragged seine of strained sea; element-fleshed,
being pure form in motion, Brancusi's fish

but never resting, had balanced so by instants;
and traveling on, taking no increment,
leaving no trace, in my sight had washed
up on a stony shore where it either vanished

and left a churn of water where it went—
like Cebes' soul a mortal occupant
of many garments and outlived by the last—

or naked continued its long journey East,

having outworn its sheaths, become pure motion,
unbroken. From the undiminished ocean
waves kept moving in, greyhounds tracking
the mechanical rabbit moon—but that one wave breaking

(and I might not see, if I had all the years
of Cebes' soul, a second wave so clear)
at my feet, happening enough, God knows, in my eyes,
if not unique, was not likely to happen twice.

POEM FOR HERMANN HESSE

Wahrlich, keiner ist weise,
Der nicht den Nebel kennt,
Der unentrinnbar und leise
Von allen ihn trennt.

i. (after *Besuch bei Hermann Hesse*)

Whatever he does seems easy, intact, a little angular—
walking with a woman, burning leaves, sitting in a ridiculous
                                                                    hat
on a stone among mountains, reading, typing a letter,
standing bemused at a door, hair awry, playing with a grand-
                                                                    child
or cat, talking with friends or a friend—and, I imagine,
simple and natural as the spreading of oak rings from an acorn
dropped into a still Spring. It would be best to age like that,
weathering down like the Appalachians into black loam
while sun after sun burned moiling fog after fog
from slopes and gentled heights dawn after dawn after dawn
until one came to believe in morning.

ii. (after 'Listening to the Wind among Pines')

The scholar sits among mountains, sleeping nearly, it seems.
                                                                    And
    everything comes to him. See! Ink-play flows into his robe,
checked by nothing, as lightning snakes to the rod. It is mist,
                                                                    though,
    locks this together—sage, waterfall, fishing-huts, warped
                                                                    pines.

A WALK IN MARCH

Somewhere near here a new-loosed creek sloughs down
to the Merrimack through dead cattails. Night slides
about the skin, blood-heat, outside,
until, years lapsed, I itch to scratch it off
and let the blackness gorging its skin balloon

blow free, be simple component of the night.
The air stinks of borning things; reborn things
roll back their stones. Spring—never easier
of access. Sixteen, we clotted at drugstore
corners evenings, watching the one some called

whore swaying her boneless body past
the hardware store, each pore and fold and chink
of flesh and fabric redolent of sin; her ass,
brassily censer-swinging, trailed a secretion
of electric musk through the elmed street.

She bore her mystery as the priest his
and we knelt openmouthed at her altar rail,
sick with ignorance. Never too old:
black calls to black yet through the straining skin.
It is the darkest night of the year, and starless.